A New True Book

FOXES

By Emilie U. Lepthien
and
Joan Kalbacken

CHILDRENS PRESS®
CHICAGO

A kit fox in its den

PHOTO CREDITS

© Reinhard Brucker—5 (2 photos), 6 (bottom left)

© Alan & Sandy Carey—Cover, 7, 17, 22, 25, 29, 39, 40

© Jerry Hennen—26

Photri—33

Root Resources—© Kenneth W. Fink, 19; © Jim Nachel, 44

Tom Stack & Associates—© Barbara Von Hoffmann, 6 (top left)

Tony Stone Images—© Hans Reinhard, 4; © Tom Ulrich, 36; © Gay Bumgarner, 45 (top)

SuperStock International, Inc.—© M. Bruce, 6 (top); © L. Rue, 10, 45 (bottom); © J. Warden, 41

Valan—© Stephen J. Krasemann, 2, 6 (bottom right), 40 bottom left); © Wayne Lankinen, 9, 14 (right), 43; © Michel Quintin, 11; © Esther Schmidt, 12, 35; © Albert Kuhnigk, 14 (left), 15 (left), 21; © B. Lyon, 15 (right); © Jeff Foott, 30; © Johnny Johnson, 38; © Dennis Schmidt, 40 (bottom right)

Visuals Unlimited—© S. Maslowski, 23; © Glenn Oliver, 27; © Will Troyer, 37

Cover: Red fox pair resting

Project Editor: Fran Dyra
Design: Margrit Fiddle

Library of Congress Cataloging-in-Publication Data

Lepthien, Emilie U. (Emilie Utteg)
    Foxes / by Emilie U. Lepthien and Joan Kalbacken.
        p.   cm. — (A New true book)
    Includes index.
    Summary: Describes the physical characteristics
and behavior of different kinds of foxes.
    ISBN 0-516-01191-X
    1. Foxes—Juvenile
literature. [1. Foxes.] I. Kalbacken, Joan.
II. Title.
QL737.C22L484   1993
599.74'442—dc20   93-3409
                                          CIP
                                          AC

TABLE OF CONTENTS

Stories about the clever fox are told in many parts of the world.

WHAT IS A FOX?

"Clever as a fox," people say. Everyone knows that foxes are very clever and cunning animals.

4

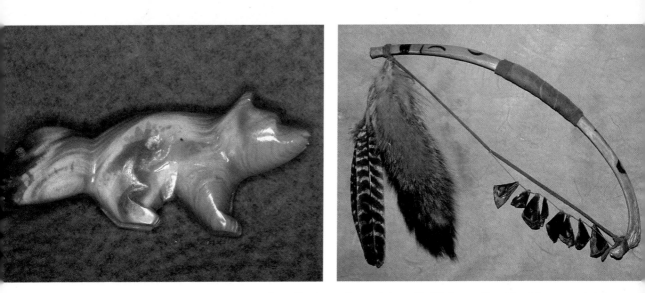

Small stone fox statue (left) from the Pueblo people
of New Mexico. A rattle of the Cheyenne Kit Fox warriors (right)
is decorated with a fox tail.

Native Americans
admired the fox for its
speed and cunning. The
Sioux and Cheyenne
called their powerful
warriors Kit Fox. The Fox
in Wisconsin were known
for their swiftness and their
ability to hunt like a fox.

5

Fox relatives include (clockwise from right) dogs, jackals, wolves, and coyotes.

Foxes are carnivores, or meat eaters. They are members of the dog family, Canidae. Dogs, wolves, coyotes, and the jackals of Asia and Africa are their relatives.

6

Foxes are found in wooded areas, forests, and farmlands. Some foxes may live in cities and suburbs.

A red fox jumps a fence in a suburban backyard.

THE RED FOX

The red fox is the most common fox. Red foxes live in North America, Europe, and Asia. They are usually reddish brown with whitish fur on their underparts.

Their outer fur has long hairs, called guard hairs, that protect the fox from rain and snow. Their soft, thick underfur keeps them

Red fox

warm in winter. This thick
underfur is shed in summer.
   The red fox has black
legs and feet and a long,
bushy tail with a white tip.
Like other foxes, except

9

The red fox's large ears help it to hear the smallest sounds.

the arctic fox, it has large ears shaped like triangles.

From its nose to its tail the red fox is about 42 inches (106 centimeters) long. It weighs from 7 to 13 pounds (3 to 6 kilograms).

This "red" fox has a silver coat.

Not all "red" foxes have reddish coats. Some are black or silver.

In the wild, red foxes may live for ten to twelve years.

A gray fox

THE GRAY FOX

The gray fox lives throughout the United States, especially in the southern states, in Mexico, Central America, and northern South America.

The gray fox has a salt-and-pepper coat with whitish underparts. Its tail has a black tip. Gray foxes are about the same size as red foxes.

Arctic fox in its summer coat (left) and in its "winter white" (right)

THE ARCTIC FOX

Arctic foxes live in the cold Arctic regions of Europe, Asia, and North America. In summer, their coat is tawny-colored. In winter, their pure-white coats make them hard to see against the snow and ice.

The thick winter fur on their pads keeps their feet warm. It also keeps them from slipping.

Arctic foxes feed on lemmings and other rodents. They also eat birds called ptarmigans and their eggs. If a dead

Arctic foxes hunt and eat ptarmigans (left) and lemmings (right).

walrus, seal, or whale is washed ashore, arctic foxes gather for a feast.

Some go out on the ice to search for food. They eat what a polar bear leaves from its seal hunt.

Like the red and gray foxes, arctic foxes do not hibernate, or sleep through the winter. Arctic foxes are about the same size as the other foxes. Their short legs, short ears, and short nose help them save body heat.

Arctic fox in winter. Its long fur protects the animal from the cold.

The scientific name for the arctic fox is *Alopex lagopus*, which means "fox with rabbit feet."

The white fur of the arctic fox and the red coat of the red fox are used to make expensive coats, jackets, and hats.

THE KIT FOX

This small fox is found in the desert regions of the western United States. The kit fox is sandy-colored and has a black-tipped tail. It is up to 31 inches (78 centimeters) long, including its tail. Kit foxes eat mice, insects, and fruit.

A kit fox. The animal's name came from "kitten,"
because of its small size.

TEETH AND TAILS

Most foxes have forty-two teeth. Foxes eat fruits and vegetables as well as insects, frogs, lizards, snakes, rabbits, and mice and other rodents. So their teeth are slightly different from other meat eaters.

Their long, sharp front teeth, called incisors, are used to catch and hold their prey. They can snip off pieces of food with

Like all predators, foxes have strong, sharp teeth.

these sharp teeth. They
also use their front teeth
to clean their beautiful fur.
Their back teeth are
flattened. Foxes crush plants
with their back teeth.
Their big, fluffy tails help
foxes keep their balance

A sleeping fox covers its nose with its tail.

when they make quick
turns. When they run, their
tail streams straight out
behind them.

When they walk, their
tail usually hangs down. A
sleeping fox uses its tail
to cover its nose and feet.

LEGS AND FEET

Foxes have long legs and they can run very fast. Few animals their size can outrun them. The gray fox can even climb a tree to escape an enemy.

When foxes trot,

Gray fox climbing a tree

they put their hind feet into the tracks of their forefeet. They can trot at 5 miles (8 kilometers) an hour for a long time.

Foxes have five toes on each forefoot and four toes on each hind foot. The fifth toe on each forefoot is a dewclaw–a small toe that does not touch the ground when foxes walk.

The sharp, curved claws on the other toes do not retract like a cat's claws. Foxes use their claws to

Red fox digging for rodents

dig their dens, bury food, and dig out rodents.

In winter, stiff hairs grow between the toe pads. These hairs help the fox to walk on slippery surfaces and also keep the feet warm.

Foxes use their teeth and tongue to remove ice from between their toes.

The fox's keen senses help it to find food and to protect itself from enemies.

KEEN SENSES

Foxes, like all doglike animals, have very sharp senses. Their eyesight is adapted to hunting at night as well as at dawn and dusk. In bright light, their pupils narrow into slits.

Red fox sniffs the air. When foxes look this shaggy, they are shedding their winter coats.

Their hearing is also excellent. Their large ears turn so that they can hear the slightest sound. A fox can hear a mouse moving in the grass 100 feet (30 meters) away.

Their sense of smell is the keenest of all. They

can smell odors 1 mile
(1.6 kilometers) away.

Foxes have several
scent glands. There is a
scent gland on each
forefoot. There are also
scent glands at the top of
the tail, and on the body
under the tail.

They use these scent
glands to mark their
territory.

Gray fox pair. Mating occurs in January or early February.

MATING

Male foxes are called dog foxes. Females are called vixens. Dog foxes use their scent to attract vixens.

A dog fox and a vixen may mate for several years or for life.

DENS

Fox homes are called dens. Some foxes dig their own dens, but many foxes enlarge a burrow that was dug by a woodchuck or a rabbit. The entrance is 8 to 12 inches (20 to 30 centimeters) wide. A tunnel slants down to about 4 feet (1.2 meters) underground.

A fox's den may be 20 to 30 feet (6 to 9 meters) long and have more than

Opposite page: Sometimes foxes make a den in a hollow log.

one entrance. If snow covers one doorway, the fox can get out through another one.

Tunnels may lead off the main den. The vixen stores extra food in these side tunnels.

Sometimes the den is hidden under brush, and sometimes the dens are made in logs or caves. Foxes keep their dens very clean.

This red fox kit is about three weeks old.

KITS ARE BORN

Halfway along the main tunnel, the vixen digs out the place where her babies, called kits, will be born. In early spring, three to six kits are born. The vixen carefully cleans her newborn kits.

Each baby in the litter weighs less than 4 ounces (113 grams). Their eyes open after about nine days.

The vixen may let the dog fox into the den after the kits' eyes are open. Otherwise he stays outside and guards the den. He also hunts for food for his mate. He leaves the food at the den entrance.

Foxes are mammals. The babies feed on their mother's milk for about five

Vixen nursing a kit

weeks after birth. Kits nurse five times a day.

When the kits are about three weeks old, small milk teeth begin to grow. But the kits continue to drink their mother's milk.

35

When the vixen can leave her litter, she joins her mate in hunting. They feed the kits with partially digested food. The parents also bring back small live prey such as mice.

The kits stay in the den for about five weeks.

Gray fox kits get a look at the world outside their den.

Young fox learning to hunt for food

GROWING UP

By midsummer, the kits
are following their father
on hunts. He teaches them
how to catch their food.

By early September the

This young arctic fox has caught a vole.

kits are ready to live on
their own. The males leave
first. Female kits stay a little
longer. Soon the mother
chases the last kits away.

COMMUNICATING

Foxes have several ways to communicate with each other. They mark places with their scent. They make sounds, too. Vixens make soft sounds as they nurse their young. The kits cry when they are hungry or lonely. Older foxes yelp and bark.

Red fox barking

Foxes can run for about one hour at a speed of 45 miles (72 kilometers) an hour. This helps them to escape when they are chased by predators such as the puma (top), the wolverine (bottom left), and the golden eagle (bottom right).

Red fox with prey

PREDATORS

Foxes are predators.
They catch and eat other
animals. But there are
predators that hunt foxes.
Bears, coyotes, pumas,
wolverines, dogs, hawks,
and eagles are their
natural enemies.

41

Foxes are nocturnal animals. They usually hunt at night. Fox trails lead to places where there are many mice and other small rodents called voles.

When foxes catch more than they can eat, they dig a hole and store the extra catch. Later, they return for the hidden food.

Farmers often kill foxes because the foxes kill

Fox burying a mouse to be eaten later

farm animals, especially chickens. However, without foxes, the numbers of mice and rats increase. So foxes may be more helpful than harmful in the farmyard.

The arctic fox's small ears help its body save heat.

FOX POPULATION

No one knows how many foxes there are today. Their numbers seem to be increasing. In many places foxes are protected by laws against hunting and trapping. In other areas, land has been set aside to provide a safe home for the clever and beautiful fox.

Foxes are protected from hunters, so their numbers are growing.

WORDS YOU SHOULD KNOW

Alopex lagopus (AL •oh •pex LAG •oh •pus) — the scientific name for the arctic fox

Canidae (KAN •ih •day) — the family of doglike animals that includes dogs, foxes, coyotes, and wolves

carnivore (KAR •nih •vor) — an animal that eats meat

dewclaw (DOO •klaw) — a short toe on the inside of an animal's front leg

digested (dih •JESS •tid) — broken down in the stomach

gland (GLAND) — a special body part that makes things that the body can use or give off

hibernate (HY •ber •nait) — to sleep through the winter

incisors (in •SY •zerz) — long, sharp front teeth

lemming (LEH •ming) — a small rodent that looks like a mouse

litter (LIT •er) — a group of baby animals all born at the same time to the same mother

mammal (MAM •il) — one of a group of warm-blooded animals that have hair and nurse their young with milk

milk teeth (MILK TEETH) — the first, small teeth of a baby animal that will later fall out and be replaced by larger permanent teeth

nocturnal (nahk •TER •nil) — active at night; hunting at night

predator (PREH •da •ter) — an animal that hunts other animals for food

prey (PRAY) — an animal that is hunted and eaten by another animal

ptarmigan (TAR •mih •gen) — a bird that is white in winter and that has feathers on its feet

retract (ree •TRAKT) — to draw back; to pull in

rodent (ROH •dint) — an animal that has long, sharp front teeth for gnawing

scientific name (sy • en • TIH • fik NAIM) — a name, usually from the Latin language, that scientists give to a plant or an animal

tawny (TAW • nee) — brownish yellow

territory (TAIR • ih • tor • ee) — an area with definite boundaries that an animal lives in

trot (TRAHT) — to run slowly

tunnel (TUH • nil) — a hole that makes a path through the ground

vixen (VIX • in) — a female fox

INDEX

About the Authors

Joan Formell Kalbacken earned a BA in education from the University of Wisconsin, Madison. After graduate work at Coe College, Iowa, and the University of Toulouse, France, she received an MA from Illinois State University, Normal, Illinois. She was a secondary school teacher in Beloit, Wisconsin, and Pekin and Normal, Illinois. She taught French and mathematics for twenty-nine years and she also served as foreign language supervisor in Normal. She received the award for excellence in Illinois' program, "Those Who Excel."

She is past state president of the Delta Kappa Gamma Society International and a member of Pi Delta Phi, Kappa Delta Pi, AAUW, and Phi Delta Kappa.

Emilie U. Lepthien received her BA and MS degrees and certificate in school administration from Northwestern University. She taught upper-grade science and social studies, wrote and narrated science programs for the Chicago Public Schools' station WBEZ, and was principal in Chicago, Illinois, for twenty years. She received the American Educator's Medal from Freedoms Foundation.

She is a member of Delta Kappa Gamma Society International, Chicago Principals' Association, Illinois Women's Press Association, National Federation of Press Women, and AAUW.

She has written books in the Enchantment of the World, New True Books, and America the Beautiful series.